Prayers with Coach

Stephanie Travis
Illustrated by Gail Travis

Published by Square Tree Publishing
www.SquareTreePublishing.com

Illustrations by: Gail Travis
Cover Graphic Artist: Sharon Marta
Editing: Monica Bosque and Shannon Saia

ISBN 978-1-7329587-8-4

Dedicated To Sunny and Cayson

May all your days be spent enjoying sports, soaking up the sun,

and sharing the joy given from the ultimate Coach, Jesus.

TABLE OF CONTENTS

When I was a child, I met Coach
for the first time.
Coach was nothing like I imagined.
Coach wanted to be my friend.

Coach was always on the sidelines and my biggest fan.
Coach always showed up.
Coach was the Ultimate Coach because, win or lose,
I knew I was loved.

Coach's Father, God, made the
biggest sacrifice for
you and me.
He sent his son, Jesus (Coach),
to take all our sins
and mistakes.

Coach teaches me so many things.
One of my favorite things Coach
taught me was how to pray.
Coach told me all I need to do is
lift my cares to Him.
No matter the situation,
Coach hears my prayer.

COACH'S PRAYER
THE LORD'S PRAYER

Our ultimate Coach, who is in Heaven, how holy is your name. Your kingdom come, your will be done, on Earth as it is in Heaven.

Give us this day only what we need, and forgive our mistakes, as you have also forgiven others who have hurt us.

Please lead us to do the right thing, and protect us from evil.

For we know Heaven will last forever, and it will always be yours because you have all the power and deserve all the glory forever and ever.

"I see you; I hear you; I know you."

CHALK TALK

1 Thessalonians 5:17 NLT
Never stop praying.

Colossians 4:2 NIV
Devote yourselves in prayer, being watchful and thankful.

1 John 5:14 NIV
This is the confidence we have in approaching God: that if we ask anything according to his will, he hears us.

Practice Plan:

Set a goal to pray (talk to Coach) as the first thing you do every morning this week.

STORY TIME

TEAMMATES

One of the best things about playing sports is that I get to make new friends every season. Some teammates have been my friends since the first season I ever played. This season, we had a new kid on our team who just moved here. He was super shy and would get very anxious at practice. My friends and I decided to have a surprise pool party after practice to help welcome him to Florida. He was a great swimmer and actually won the game Sharks and Minnows!

TEAMMATES
PRAYER FOR FRIENDS

Dear Coach,

Thank you for the friends you have placed in my life. Help me accept and love them as you love me. Thank you for giving me people to play with, laugh with, and provide comfort to. Help me to be a good friend to others and look for ways to be a blessing in return.

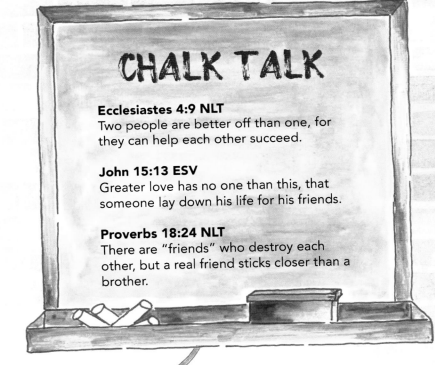

CHALK TALK

Ecclesiastes 4:9 NLT
Two people are better off than one, for they can help each other succeed.

John 15:13 ESV
Greater love has no one than this, that someone lay down his life for his friends.

Proverbs 18:24 NLT
There are "friends" who destroy each other, but a real friend sticks closer than a brother.

"Rely on me for strength and control."

Practice Plan:

Invite a friend to go to a local park, your house, or a field, and play a game you both enjoy.

STORY TIME
WARM UP

One of my favorite things to do is play basketball with my dad. As soon as he gets home from work, he hurries up and changes so we can go play. My dad always helps me work on things that I need to practice for the games. One of these things happens to be foul shots. I get so nervous in a game when I have to take them because everyone is watching me. The gym gets quiet. It is just me, the basketball, and the hoop. One thing my dad encourages me to do is to take a deep breath, imagine it going in, and ask God for courage. I try to do this every time, and even if the ball doesn't go in, the butterflies become still.

WARM UP

PRAYER FOR WHEN YOU FEEL ANXIOUS

Dear Coach,

Please help me to be calm and do my best. Please help me remember to just breathe, and let all the butterflies be still in my tummy. Thank you for caring about me. Please put peace in my heart, and help me always remember to trust in you.

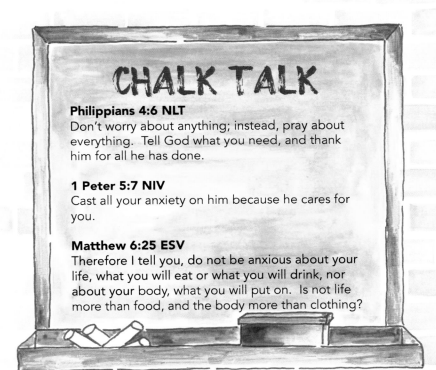

CHALK TALK

Philippians 4:6 NLT
Don't worry about anything; instead, pray about everything. Tell God what you need, and thank him for all he has done.

1 Peter 5:7 NIV
Cast all your anxiety on him because he cares for you.

Matthew 6:25 ESV
Therefore I tell you, do not be anxious about your life, what you will eat or what you will drink, nor about your body, what you will put on. Is not life more than food, and the body more than clothing?

"Give me your worries because I care for you."

Practice Plan:

Take five deep breaths and say, "Be still and know that I am God."

STORY TIME
COACH'S CALL

Once in a while, I will try to just do things my way. I don't trust that my P.E. coach is teaching me how to do a skill right. I try to do it my own way, but I end up getting more upset and frustrated with what I am doing. When this happens, my P.E. coach can always tell. That is when I know I need to apologize and focus on what the coach is teaching me and trust that he knows what is best for me.

COACH'S CALL
PRAYER FOR TRUSTING GOD

Dear Coach,

Thank you for creating me to be on your team. Help me to listen to you and read your playbook (Bible) when I don't understand the situation. You are my strength and shield. Guide me to trust in your perfect timing.

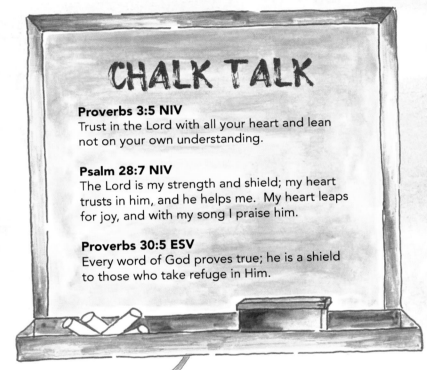

CHALK TALK

Proverbs 3:5 NIV
Trust in the Lord with all your heart and lean not on your own understanding.

Psalm 28:7 NIV
The Lord is my strength and shield; my heart trusts in him, and he helps me. My heart leaps for joy, and with my song I praise him.

Proverbs 30:5 ESV
Every word of God proves true; he is a shield to those who take refuge in Him.

"I am taking today and using it for tomorrow."

Practice Plan:

What is one thing you need to trust Coach with today?

STORY TIME
WEARING THE UNIFORM

One of my favorite parts about playing football is the uniform! I am honored that I get to play for one of the best teams in the town. I feel unstoppable when I put on my pads and armor up in my helmet. After the game, my family and teammates love to get ice cream. Sometimes we get a little rowdy and make a mess and forget that there are other people in the ice cream shop. Our coach always reminds us that when wearing our uniform jerseys, we are not just representing ourselves, we are representing our team.

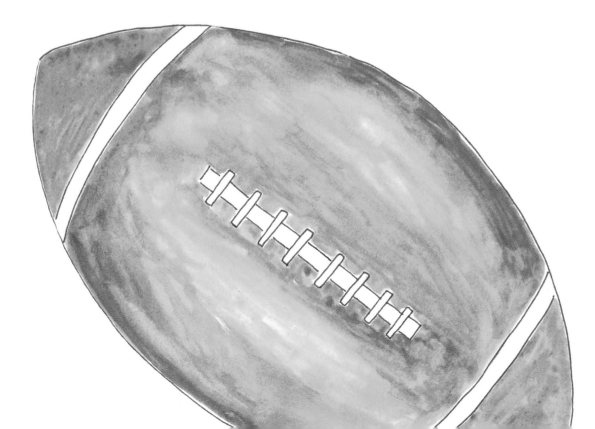

WEARING THE UNIFORM
PRAYER FOR INTEGRITY

Dear Coach,

Help me to make good choices, even when no one is looking. Help me to choose what is right and not what is easiest for me. Give me opportunities that will grow my character.

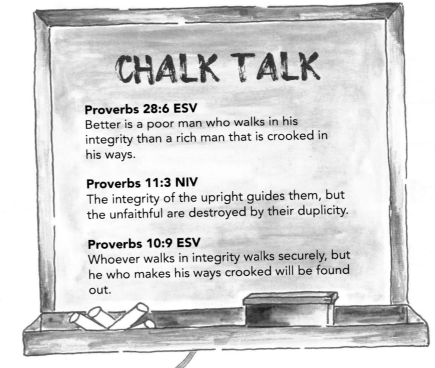

CHALK TALK

Proverbs 28:6 ESV
Better is a poor man who walks in his integrity than a rich man that is crooked in his ways.

Proverbs 11:3 NIV
The integrity of the upright guides them, but the unfaithful are destroyed by their duplicity.

Proverbs 10:9 ESV
Whoever walks in integrity walks securely, but he who makes his ways crooked will be found out.

"Cling to my spirit for direction."

Practice Plan:

Practice making good choices when no one is with you. Clean your room without your parents asking, write an apology note if you've done something wrong, spend extra time praying, or start your homework early.

STORY TIME
TOO MUCH EQUIPMENT

My mom loves when I have a clean bedroom. She loves it even more when I try to clean it up myself. Lately, I am finding I have nowhere to put all my athletic shoes and balls. They seem to be exploding out of my toy bin and closet. My sister had a great idea. We would bag up our extra equipment and old athletic shoes and donate them to someone in need because we have too much stuff.

TOO MUCH EQUIPMENT
PRAYER FOR POSSESSIONS

Dear Coach,

I am feeling like I have too much stuff in my life. Help me to look for opportunities to give to those in need. I know I don't need all my earthly treasures and some are just desires. Help me to invest my money and time in things that are eternal.

CHALK TALK

Mark 8:36 ESV
For what does it profit a man to gain the whole world and forfeit his soul?

Luke 18:22 ESV
When Jesus heard this, he said to him, "One thing you still lack. Sell all that you have and distribute to the poor, and you will have treasure in heaven; and come, follow me.

Matthew 6:20 NIV
But store up for yourselves treasures in heaven, where moths and vermin do not destroy, and where thieves do not break in and steal.

"Invest in a relationship with me."

Practice Plan:

Grab an empty bag and fill it with things that you can give to those in need.

STORY TIME
PRACTICE CANCELLED

I love to play tennis. Most days, I will play before school when the sun rises and then even at nighttime under the court's lights. I sometimes lose track of time and get super tired because I want to be the best I can be. When that happens, my elbow will usually start hurting. My dad always tells me that I have to listen to my body. When my elbow hurts, I need to rest and ice it. Then, I need to be still and listen to God till I am better.

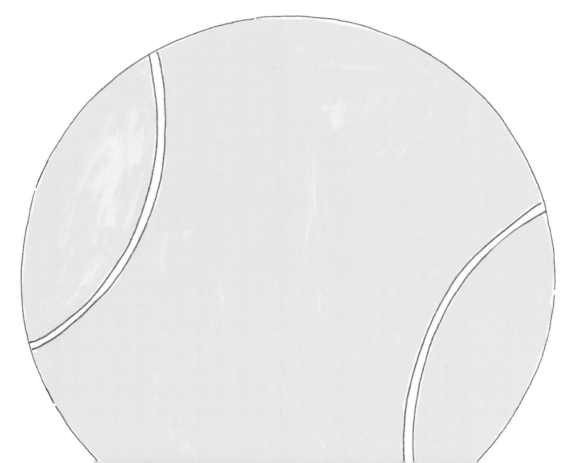

PRACTICE CANCELLED
PRAYER FOR REST

Dear Coach,

Thank you for giving me the ability to play sports. Right now, I am tired and need you to carry me. Help me to rest in your peace and slow down so I can hear your voice. When I am weary and exhausted, help me to find my rest in you.

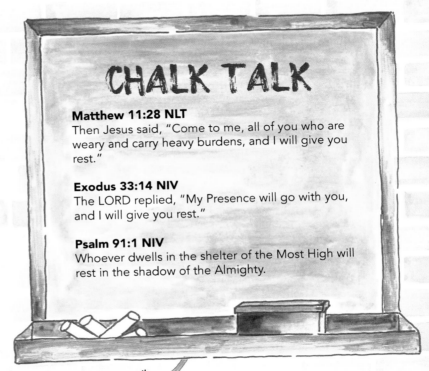

CHALK TALK

Matthew 11:28 NLT
Then Jesus said, "Come to me, all of you who are weary and carry heavy burdens, and I will give you rest."

Exodus 33:14 NIV
The LORD replied, "My Presence will go with you, and I will give you rest."

Psalm 91:1 NIV
Whoever dwells in the shelter of the Most High will rest in the shadow of the Almighty.

"When you don't see your footprints, that is when I carry you."

Practice Plan:

Take five minutes and go somewhere you like to rest and be still with Coach.

STORY TIME

PEP TALK

It is so thrilling when I get a hit in a ball game. The ball flies off of the bat, fans cheer, and my teammates jump up and down in excitement. Unfortunately, it doesn't always happen that way. Once in a while, it happens—I strikeout. It's almost as if I forget how to hit the ball! That's when the coach calls me over and gives me an encouraging pep talk. The coach usually tells me to have confidence and to keep doing my best.

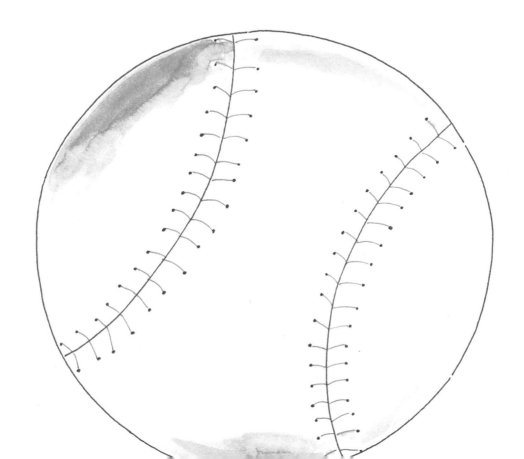

PEP TALK
PRAYER FOR ENCOURAGEMENT

Dear Coach,

Thank you that I can just talk to you when I am feeling overwhelmed. I am having a hard time staying focused and believing in myself. Please help me to stay positive and hold on to joy in tough times.

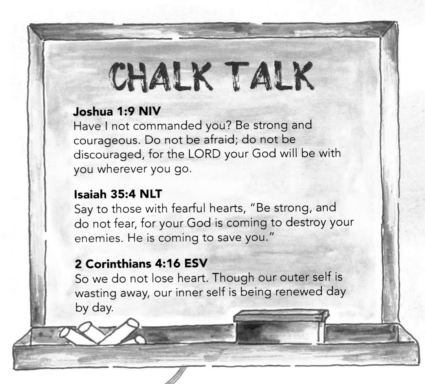

CHALK TALK

Joshua 1:9 NIV
Have I not commanded you? Be strong and courageous. Do not be afraid; do not be discouraged, for the LORD your God will be with you wherever you go.

Isaiah 35:4 NLT
Say to those with fearful hearts, "Be strong, and do not fear, for your God is coming to destroy your enemies. He is coming to save you."

2 Corinthians 4:16 ESV
So we do not lose heart. Though our outer self is wasting away, our inner self is being renewed day by day.

"I bring you courage and hope."

Practice Plan:

Read the "Chalk Talk" scripture Joshua 1:9 to yourself in a mirror or say it out loud three times.

STORY TIME
TEAM CAPTAIN

When my teammates get discouraged in a game, it can be easy to give up, especially if others around me are starting to have negative thoughts. Then the team captain usually steps up and leads the team. They do such a great job of getting everyone to think positive and not to give up. I always think the team captain is so brave when they do that.

TEAM CAPTAIN
PRAYER FOR LEADERSHIP

Dear Coach,

Thank you for the people you have placed in my life to lead and to mentor me. Please help me to encourage my friends by being a good example. Help me to include everyone, to listen well, and to always try my best.

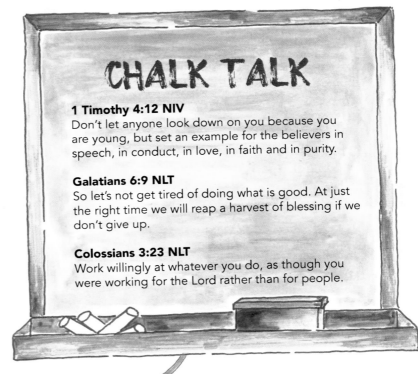

CHALK TALK

1 Timothy 4:12 NIV
Don't let anyone look down on you because you are young, but set an example for the believers in speech, in conduct, in love, in faith and in purity.

Galatians 6:9 NLT
So let's not get tired of doing what is good. At just the right time we will reap a harvest of blessing if we don't give up.

Colossians 3:23 NLT
Work willingly at whatever you do, as though you were working for the Lord rather than for people.

"No matter your age, you can be a leader."

Practice Plan:

Write down three words that describe a leader.

STORY TIME

OBEYING THE WHISTLE

My favorite part about school is recess. I count down the minutes in my head for the bell to ring so we can go play football. We tend to lose self-control even just lining up because we are so excited! My friends and I usually play well together, and we follow the rules of two-hand touch. Sometimes though, a player will get mad and try to tackle someone. This usually ends our game, and a player ends up crying because someone lost self-control. When this happens, the teacher pulls us together and disciplines us.

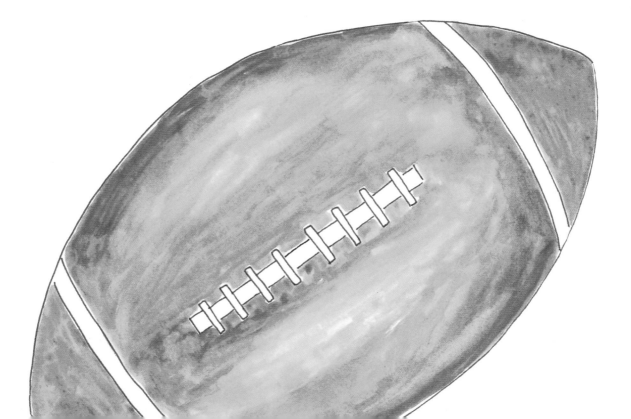

OBEYING THE WHISTLE

PRAYER FOR SELF-CONTROL

Dear Coach,

Sometimes I struggle with controlling my temper. I know this is not pleasing to you. Please help me to control my words, hands, and feet. Protect and guide me to find a better answer that will bring glory to you.

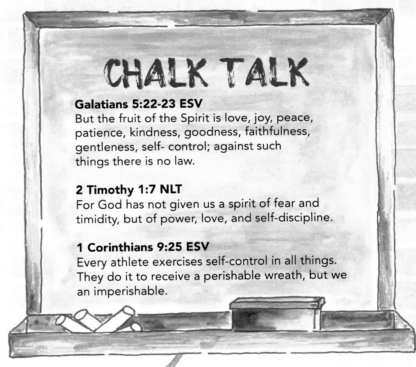

CHALK TALK

Galatians 5:22-23 ESV
But the fruit of the Spirit is love, joy, peace, patience, kindness, goodness, faithfulness, gentleness, self- control; against such things there is no law.

2 Timothy 1:7 NLT
For God has not given us a spirit of fear and timidity, but of power, love, and self-discipline.

1 Corinthians 9:25 ESV
Every athlete exercises self-control in all things. They do it to receive a perishable wreath, but we an imperishable.

"Rely on me for strength and control."

Practice Plan:

The next time you get upset with friends, take a time-out and regain control of your feelings.

STORY TIME
HUDDLE TIME

Playing a team sport is very exciting. I always make new friends during the season and laugh like crazy. Sometimes our coach has to talk to us if we are goofing around more than playing. Though we all want to be the all-star on the court, we play so much better when we work as a team, listen, and carry out our plays together.

HUDDLE TIME

PRAYER FOR TEAM

Dear Coach,

Thank you for my team. Thank you for the coaches and teachers that love us and teach us wisdom. Please help us to have patience with each other and work together as a team. Please guide my team to make decisions that bring you joy.

"We are stronger together."

CHALK TALK

1 Thessalonians 5:11 ESV
Therefore encourage one another and build one another up, just as you are doing.

Matthew 17:20 NIV
He replied, "Because you have so little faith. Truly I tell you, if you have faith as small as a mustard seed, you can say to this mountain, 'Move from here to there,' and it will move. Nothing will be impossible for you."

Ephesians 4:3 NIV
Make every effort to keep the unity of the Spirit through the bond of peace.

Practice Plan:

Ask God what is something you could say to your friends/teammates to encourage them to work together.

STORY TIME

TIME OUT

Playing soccer on a muddy field can be a lot of fun. The only trouble is sometimes it's hard to see if there are holes in the grass. One time, I twisted my ankle so bad that it swelled up to the size of my knee! It was very sore, and I was not able to play for three weeks until my ankle healed.

TIME OUT
PRAYER FOR HEALING

Dear Coach,

Thank you for all the miracles you have already preformed. You made me and you know what is best for me. Please come and comfort me and begin healing me from the inside out. Thank you for giving me friends and family to care for me. Please help me remember you are always by my side.

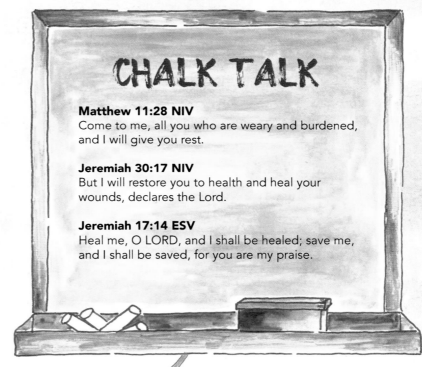

CHALK TALK

Matthew 11:28 NIV
Come to me, all you who are weary and burdened, and I will give you rest.

Jeremiah 30:17 NIV
But I will restore you to health and heal your wounds, declares the Lord.

Jeremiah 17:14 ESV
Heal me, O LORD, and I shall be healed; save me, and I shall be saved, for you are my praise.

"I will restore you to health and heal your wounds."

Practice Plan:

Thank Coach for all the ways He has already healed you when you were hurting. Pray that He will do it again.

STORY TIME
HALFTIME

Last season, my team lost the first three games in a row. I noticed we started to get upset with each other about the 3rd inning in the games when things were not going our way. We began to walk up to bat with our heads hanging low, and we would stop encouraging our pitcher and field players. That's when coach would step in and say,
"Who is going to step up and lead this team today?"

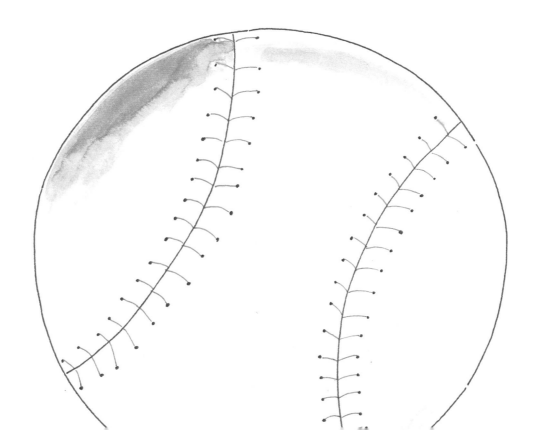

HALFTIME

PRAYER FOR DETERMINATION

Dear Coach,

Thank you that I am able to play in this game. Help me to remember that even when it gets challenging, you will be with me through it all. Please help me to not give up and to use game experiences to help me be a good role model for you.

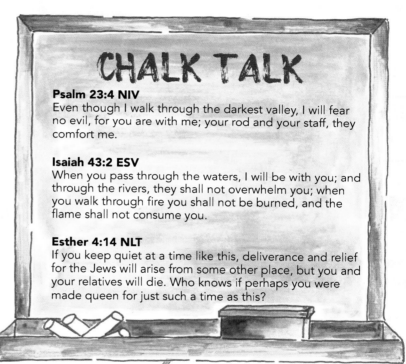

CHALK TALK

Psalm 23:4 NIV
Even though I walk through the darkest valley, I will fear no evil, for you are with me; your rod and your staff, they comfort me.

Isaiah 43:2 ESV
When you pass through the waters, I will be with you; and through the rivers, they shall not overwhelm you; when you walk through fire you shall not be burned, and the flame shall not consume you.

Esther 4:14 NLT
If you keep quiet at a time like this, deliverance and relief for the Jews will arise from some other place, but you and your relatives will die. Who knows if perhaps you were made queen for just such a time as this?

...d fast to me in this season and be determined to press on."

Practice Plan:

Take a "Halftime Water Break" to refuel your body, soul, and spirit and be determined to finish strong.

STORY TIME

SPORTSMANSHIP

This year I had to play my best friend in the biggest tennis tournament in our town. She is my practice partner, and we play almost every day after school. We love to play against each other in practice. We love to challenge each other. We love to laugh, as well, when something silly happens. When we played against each other in the tournament, she won the last set. We both played very hard, but she still won. I was very upset when I should have been happy for her.

SPORTSMANSHIP

PRAYER FOR CHEERING ON OTHERS

Dear Coach,

Thank you for my voice. Thank you that I am able to use my words to encourage and bless others. Please help me to control my body language and temper. Guide me to be happy for others when they succeed.

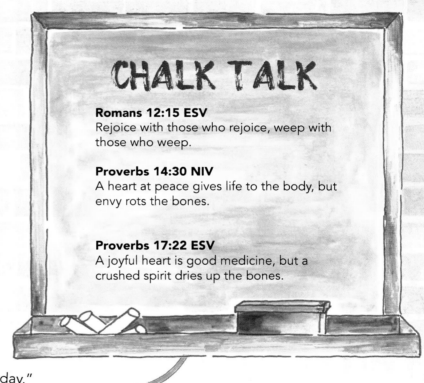

CHALK TALK

Romans 12:15 ESV
Rejoice with those who rejoice, weep with those who weep.

Proverbs 14:30 NIV
A heart at peace gives life to the body, but envy rots the bones.

Proverbs 17:22 ESV
A joyful heart is good medicine, but a crushed spirit dries up the bones.

"A cheerful heart is like a sunny day."

Practice Plan:

Look for an opportunity to cheer on others and show respect during an event.

STORY TIME

EXTRA FITNESS

I was sick the whole week before my last football game. Though I was feeling much better by game night, there was no power in my throws when I was playing quarterback. My hands felt shaky, and my energy level was super low. As I sat on the bench between plays, I decided to pray and ask for help. When I did that, I knew I wasn't fighting alone in this game!

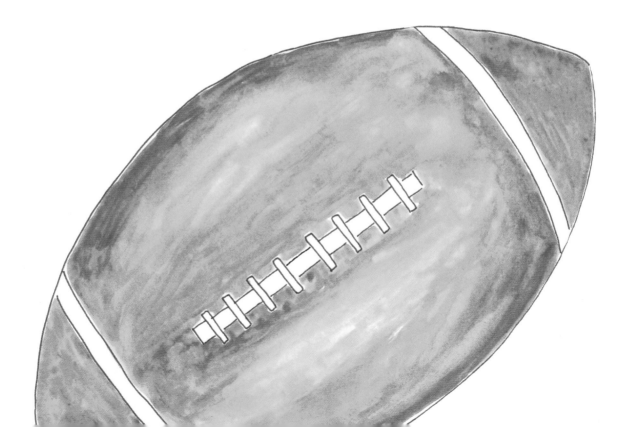

EXTRA FITNESS
PRAYER FOR STRENGTH

Dear Coach,

Thank you that we can call on you for power. Please give me strength for today. Please renew my mind, body, and soul. Give me the power to keep working hard and doing my best. Please remind me that all my strength comes from you and is used to bring glory to your name.

CHALK TALK

Philippians 4:13 NIV
I can do all this through him who gives me strength.

Isaiah 40:31 NLT
But those who trust in the LORD will find new strength. They will soar high on wings like eagles. They will run and not grow weary. They will walk and not faint.

Psalm 28:7 ESV
The LORD is my strength and my shield; in him my heart trusts, and I am helped; my heart exults, and with my song I give thanks to him.

"Put on your armor and fight the good fight."

Practice Plan:

Create an exercise plan to strengthen your body.

STORY TIME

SHARING THE GAME

Backyard soccer is so much fun. People from all over the neighborhood will come and play. One time, we had so many people on the field the ball was just flying everywhere. Someone happened to kick the ball so hard it flew far too deep into the bushes for us to retrieve. My friend, who brought the ball, began crying because that was the only soccer ball he had. So, I went in the garage and gave him one of my extra soccer balls.

SHARING THE GAME

PRAYER FOR GENEROSITY

Dear Coach,

Thank you for the things you have already given me. Help me to let go of my extra things and give them freely to whomever is in need. Guide me in looking for ways to give and do it with a grateful heart. Thank you for all the blessings. Thank you for sharing your son Jesus with us.

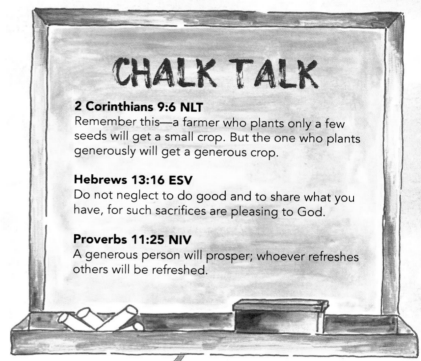

CHALK TALK

2 Corinthians 9:6 NLT
Remember this—a farmer who plants only a few seeds will get a small crop. But the one who plants generously will get a generous crop.

Hebrews 13:16 ESV
Do not neglect to do good and to share what you have, for such sacrifices are pleasing to God.

Proverbs 11:25 NIV
A generous person will prosper; whoever refreshes others will be refreshed.

"Nothing is greater than giving with a grateful heart."

Practice Plan:

Give someone an extra ball or sports equipment that you could do without and teach them a trick or something fun to do with it.

STORY TIME

BAD CALL

Playing volleyball at the beach with my friends is super exciting; however, it can be distracting at times. There can be dolphins jumping, birds flying, the sun setting and people surfing, all while we are playing. One time, my friend was serving the ball and it hit my head because I was looking the other way! I got so upset with her that I told her I didn't want to play with her anymore.

BAD CALL
PRAYER FOR FORGIVENESS

Dear Coach,

Thank you for loving me no matter what. Please forgive me for what I did. Please help me to ask for forgiveness from whomever needs to hear it and take responsibility for my own actions. Give me strength to make better choices. Thank you for forgiving us.

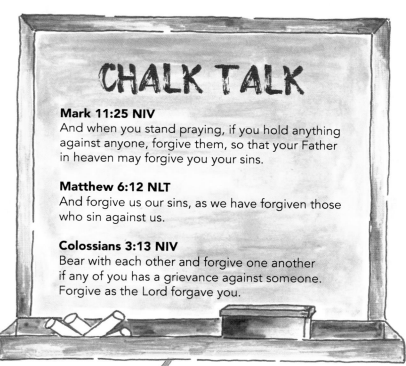

CHALK TALK

Mark 11:25 NIV
And when you stand praying, if you hold anything against anyone, forgive them, so that your Father in heaven may forgive you your sins.

Matthew 6:12 NLT
And forgive us our sins, as we have forgiven those who sin against us.

Colossians 3:13 NIV
Bear with each other and forgive one another if any of you has a grievance against someone. Forgive as the Lord forgave you.

"Look up and let go of anything you are gripping too tightly."

Practice Plan:

Draw a picture or write a letter to someone from whom you need to ask forgiveness.

STORY TIME

COMPETITION

There is this one team that I never like to play. They don't always seem to play by the rules, and they can have a bad attitude if they start losing. It makes me want to be rude to them and say mean things because they hurt my feelings. When this happens, I get so flustered that I lose my care for the game. These are the times when I really need to pray for them, but it's hard.

COMPETITION
PRAYER FOR OUR ENEMIES

Dear Coach,

Thank you that you give us tough situations to make us stronger. Please help me when I get angry, frustrated, and jealous. Show me how to want the best for others just as you want the best for me. Please keep them safe and give us both grace and humility to live in peace with each other.

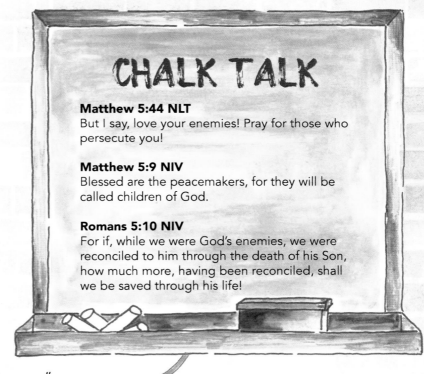

CHALK TALK

Matthew 5:44 NLT
But I say, love your enemies! Pray for those who persecute you!

Matthew 5:9 NIV
Blessed are the peacemakers, for they will be called children of God.

Romans 5:10 NIV
For if, while we were God's enemies, we were reconciled to him through the death of his Son, how much more, having been reconciled, shall we be saved through his life!

"Love my players, just as I love you."

Practice Plan:

The next time you are in a competitive situation, encourage your competition by saying something kind to them.

STORY TIME

LOSING THE GAME

We worked all season to play in the championship game. We practiced, we planned, and we got pumped up for the big day. Friends and family cheered us on with big posters and cowbells. The game was really close untill the last quarter. The other team pulled ahead, and we were never able to catch back up. We lost. My teammates were very upset after the game, so we decided to meet the next day for a fun scrimmage together to shake off the big loss.

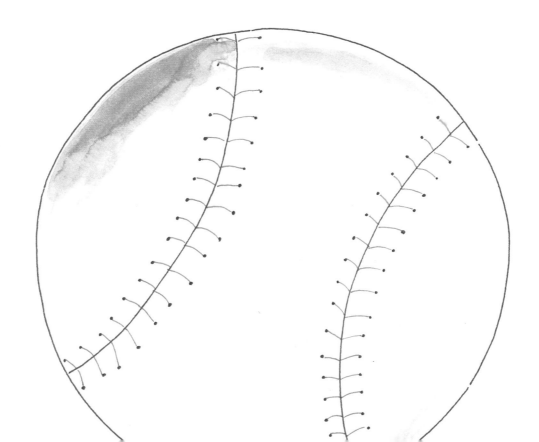

LOSING THE GAME
PRAYER WHEN YOU FEEL SAD

Dear Coach,

Thank you for being close to those that are hurting. Today I am feeling sad and maybe don't even know fully why. Please comfort me and help me to have hope in my situation.

CHALK TALK

Psalm 34:17 NLT
The LORD hears his people when they call to him for help. He rescues them from all their troubles.

Matthew 5:4 NIV
Blessed are those who mourn, for they will be comforted.

2 Corinthians 1:4 NLT
He comforts us in all our troubles so that we can comfort others. When they are troubled, we will be able to give them the same comfort God has given us.

"I bring you comfort on all sides during your time of need."

Practice Plan:

Draw a picture of something you like that makes you smile.

STORY TIME

CELEBRATING THE WIN

My birthday this year fell on a Saturday during volleyball season. We were playing against the toughest team we faced that season. I was pretty nervous going in because the last thing I wanted to happen was to lose on my birthday! What was so neat is, we won! Not only did we win on my birthday, but I was also thankful for my mom, who brought a birthday cake, so my whole team got to celebrate with me!

CELEBRATING THE WIN

PRAYER WHEN THANKFUL

Dear Coach,

Thank you for creating me and the gifts and talents you have given me. Thank you for trusting me to carry out your plans. Help me to always rejoice with you on my wins. When I receive praise from others, remind me to point it all right back at you.

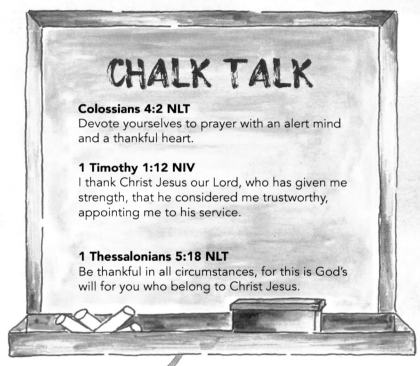

CHALK TALK

Colossians 4:2 NLT
Devote yourselves to prayer with an alert mind and a thankful heart.

1 Timothy 1:12 NIV
I thank Christ Jesus our Lord, who has given me strength, that he considered me trustworthy, appointing me to his service.

1 Thessalonians 5:18 NLT
Be thankful in all circumstances, for this is God's will for you who belong to Christ Jesus.

"I have gifted you to do great things for the Kingdom."

Practice Plan:

Think of 5 to 10 things you are thankful for and write them down.

STORY TIME
OVERTIME

Surfing can be really hard when the waves are big. Some days, I can hardly paddle out! On those days, I remind myself that once I get past where the wave breaks, it will be calm again. That is when I sit on the board, take a break, and enjoy the reward of not giving up.

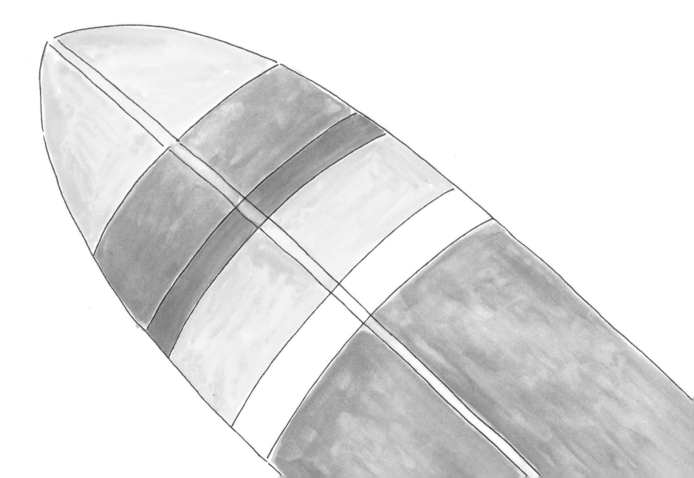

OVERTIME
PRAYER FOR PERSEVERANCE

Dear Coach,

Thank you for giving me new mercies each day. Help me to finish strong in all that you have for me. Please help me to keep my eyes on you and trust the process. I know that with you, all things are possible, and I can do hard things.

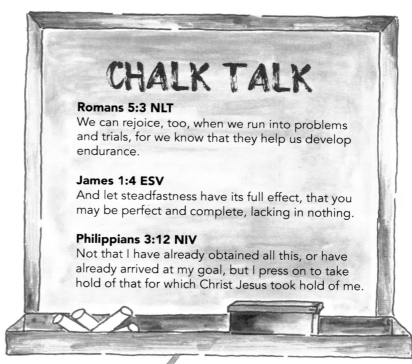

CHALK TALK

Romans 5:3 NLT
We can rejoice, too, when we run into problems and trials, for we know that they help us develop endurance.

James 1:4 ESV
And let steadfastness have its full effect, that you may be perfect and complete, lacking in nothing.

Philippians 3:12 NIV
Not that I have already obtained all this, or have already arrived at my goal, but I press on to take hold of that for which Christ Jesus took hold of me.

"Press on to win the prize of eternal life."

Practice Plan:

Tell someone about something really hard that you did and why it was worth it to push through and keep going (like riding a bike).

STORY TIME
GOOD GAME

My friends and I love playing sports together after school. It really doesn't matter what sport it is. We just meet at the field, and we usually take a vote. Today, football won the vote, and it just so happens to be my worst sport. In the first play of the game I fumbled the ball, and everyone began to give me a hard time. I had to remind myself that we all make mistakes.

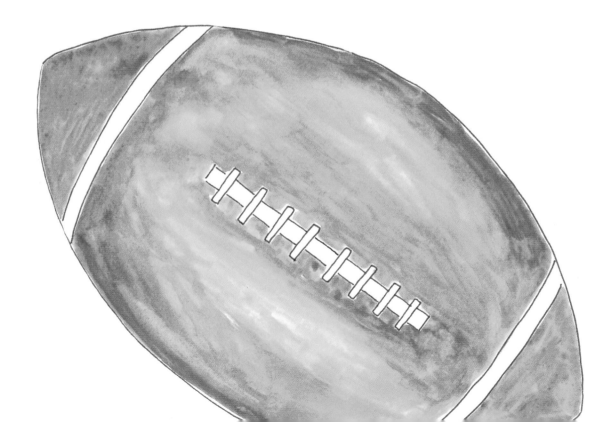

GOOD GAME

PRAYER FOR HUMILITY

Dear Coach,

Thank you for showing your love for me even when I feel unlovable. Thank you for all the blessings that you provide for me. Help me to always put you first and think of others before myself, just as Jesus did for us. Help me to see any pride in my life and lay it down before you.

"Stay grounded with a heart of gratitude."

CHALK TALK

1 Peter 5:6 NLT
So humble yourselves under the mighty power of God, and at the right time he will lift you up in honor.

Matthew 11:29 NIV
Take my yoke upon you and learn from me, for I am gentle and humble in heart, and you will find rest for your souls.

Colossians 3:12 NIV
Therefore, as God's chosen people, holy and dearly loved, clothe yourselves with compassion, kindness, humility, gentleness and patience.

Practice Plan:

Think of a person you can do something special for.
Now go do just that!

STORY TIME
FINISHING STRONG

Towards the end of the game, you can usually see which team has a higher fitness level. One game, in particular, went into overtime, and both of our teams were extremely tired. You could see that in our faces and in how slowly we were moving. All of a sudden, in the last three minutes of overtime, the players on my team who were not in the game became full of energy and started encouraging us. We scored in the last 30 seconds and won! It took the whole team to win that game and not give up.

FINISHING STRONG
PRAYER FOR ENDURANCE

Dear Coach,

Thank you for giving me energy to play. Thank you for space to play, air to breathe, and friends to play with. Help me to press in and be persistent in working at my best. Guide me to listen, grow, and push through to the next season you have in store for me.

CHALK TALK

1 Corinthians 9:24 ESV
Do you not know that in a race all the runners run, but only one receives the prize? So run that you may obtain it.

John 19:30 NIV
When he had received the drink, Jesus said, "It is finished." With that, he bowed his head and gave up his spirit.

Hebrews 12:7 NIV
Endure hardship as discipline; God is treating you as his children. For what children are not disciplined by their father?

"For I have finished the work and given you freedom."

Practice Plan:

Do interval training for 5 to 10 minutes, three times per week. Walk for 30 seconds, then run for 30 seconds.

STORY TIME
THE COMEBACK

The day Coach came into my heart for the first time is a day I will never forget. It was almost as if I could hear angels celebrating like fans on the sidelines. My heart smiled deep that day, and I was so excited to spend more time learning about Coach's playbook, the Bible. He gave me the ultimate game plan: love Coach and love His Players.

THE COMEBACK
THE SINNER'S PRAYER

Dear Coach,

I know that you made me, and you created me to be with you. I have disobeyed you and done things my way. Thank you for sending your son, Jesus, to take away my sins. I ask that you please save me and come live in my heart and be the ultimate Life Coach over me.

CHALK TALK

John 3:16 NIV

For God so loved the world that he gave his one and only Son, that whoever believes in him shall not perish but have eternal life.

"Now go and make disciples."

Practice Plan:

Write down the date that you met Coach for the first time and asked Him to come live in your heart forever.

Stephanie Travis, Author

Stephanie Travis grew up on the east coast of Florida, living out her passion for sports, the ocean, and adventure. Today, she and her husband Jay reside in Bradenton, Florida with their two children, Sunny and Cayson.

Since graduating from Florida State University, Stephanie has taught physical education and life skills for fourteen years. She has coached countless seasons of sports, including soccer, softball, volleyball, and weightlifting teams.

Stephanie is well-versed in fitness and is a personal trainer, wholeness coach, and the owner of Groundswell surf school, a summer surf school for elementary-aged children.

Stephanie's passion for wellness has led her to advocate for human trafficking prevention education. She travels globally (from Texas to South Africa) to share human trafficking awareness strategies to equip educators to reach students. Stephanie believes every life has value, and everyone needs a COACH.

Gail Travis, Illustrator

Gail Travis has been creating art since she was five years old. After finishing college in Ohio for commercial art, she packed up her car and traveled south to the land of surf and sunshine, Florida. Gail co-owned a very successful advertising agency with a dear friend, which led to her next venture, "Noah's Art," a company specializing in children's art and murals.

In her free time, Gail enjoys painting in watercolors, acrylics, and oils. Her artwork has been available for purchase in various locations across the west coast of Florida. She loves tennis, sailing, kayaking, and just being outside in God's nature.

Her six beloved grandchildren affectionately know her as Nina.

Made in the USA
Columbia, SC
25 November 2020